BASIC TOPIARY

A Living Approach

Dean & Geraldine Myers

Schiffer Publishing Ltd®

4880 Lower Valley Road, Atglen, Pennsylvania 19310

Other Schiffer Books on Related Subjects:

Copyright © 2010 by Dean & Geraldine Myers
Technical support: Genise Wade
Graphics© 2010 by Wesley Flear

Library of Congress Control Number: 2010926858

Type set in Zurich BT

ISBN: 978-0-7643-3634-8
Printed in China

Schiffer Books are available at special discounts for bulk purchases for sales promotions or premiums. Special editions, including personalized covers, corporate imprints, and excerpts can be created in large quantities for special needs. For more information contact the publisher:

Published by Schiffer Publishing Ltd.
4880 Lower Valley Road
Atglen, PA 19310
Phone: (610) 593-1777; Fax: (610) 593-2002
E-mail: Info@schifferbooks.com

For the largest selection of fine reference books on this and related subjects, please visit our web site at
www.schifferbooks.com
We are always looking for people to write books on new and related subjects. If you have an idea for a book please contact us at the above address.

This book may be purchased from the publisher.
Include $5.00 for shipping.
Please try your bookstore first.
You may write for a free catalog.

In Europe, Schiffer books are distributed by
Bushwood Books
6 Marksbury Ave.
Kew Gardens
Surrey TW9 4JF England
Phone: 44 (0) 20 8392 8585; Fax: 44 (0) 20 8392 9876
E-mail: info@bushwoodbooks.co.uk
Website: www.bushwoodbooks.co.uk

Contents

The Living
Approach to Topiary

All my life I have been interested in gardening and landscaping. I started by arranging garden plants and vegetables in the back yard of my childhood home.

I have also always been an artist—drawing, painting, and arranging styles and forms. With an artist's eye I observed people growing different vines and other plants on arbors, the foliage climbing up a wooden form against a wall or standing free. As I walked through the woods, I noticed that, even in nature, plants would sometimes take on unnatural positions and shapes when they were stressed or met with obstacles like fallen trees or rocks. They were amazingly adaptable and continued to grow without harm. The artist in me asked, "Why can't I use this natural tendency to create a new work of art, a living statue of sorts?"

That was really the genesis of the methods shared in this book. Think of a bush as a balloon or a columned bundle of bendable grass or reeds—the kind you could use to make a basket or a wicker chair. If you can visualize this, you probably have the ability to follow these instructions well. Visualizing your final product is half the battle.

7 Steps to Topiary

There are seven steps to your success:

1. Select a design you like. Keep in mind the dimensions (height and width) of the bush.

2. Access the bush and check the structure. See where it is sparse and where it has older, unbendable parts on the inside. If they will interfere with the design, trim them out. Some stronger, unbendable parts may remain and be used for support and to tie off other parts of the plant.

3. Section the bush according to the design.

4. Tie off the sections and secure.

5. Trim and shape to show details of the overall design.

6. Wait for regrowth, then tuck new growth into the topiary to reshape and fill.

7. Trim new growth repeatedly. You can also use some new growth to add to the design. In the projects shared in this book, new growth will help to improve the feathers, head, and beak of the peacock or to perfect the dress, wings, head, and arms of the angel.

Tools You'll Need

Hedge shears – useful for trimming or shaping hedges. There is not a lot of heavy trimming so regular garden trimmers should be fine. One of the blades might be notched to help cut larger twigs and branches. Some trimmers have shock absorbing cushioned bumpers to reduce jarring and forearm fatigue.

Loppers – these larger, long-handled cutters are helpful when working with thorny branches. You can also find these with shock absorbing cushioned bumpers.

Pole pruners – a long pole usually equipped with a rope-operated clipper and a saw. Some poles telescope, giving them more flexibility. Make sure the pole remains sturdy even at its longer lengths so it will be useful for high trimming.

String or rope – used for tying off the bush, this needs to be strong enough for the job. Lighter string is fine for a small plant, but heavier rope may be necessary for a large bush. Sometimes you can find this in green or another dark color, which helps camouflage it.

Fundamentals of Making Topiaries

Remember that you can create topiary out of almost any bush. Just as a painter uses a paintbrush or a carver a knife or chisel, you are using string and trimmers to create your works of art.

While some topiaries use a wire form to support them, in this technique the bush itself is the form and there is no need for any additional support.

Because of this, in the beginning the bush may not have the particular shape or fullness you desire. At that point, the bush is just an undeveloped work of art. When foliage develops or re-grows and fills in the skeleton you have formed, your topiary turns into a true "living image."

Several different plants can be used for the same form. While the demonstration peacock and angel topiaries were made from an azalea bush, there is an example of a large peacock and angel that were made from California Privets. In the step-by-step studio project, the duck used a Rheingold Aborvitae. The larger outside ducks were made out of barberry bushes. I use Sky Pencils in the studio to show how to make Gothic arches, but in the yard I have used hibiscus bushes for the same form.

In short, you can use this topiary technique on any hedge bush, including evergreen bushes. Evergreens do not shed their foliage like privet shrubs, hibiscus, barberry, and forsythia bushes. With so many options, you may be able to consider creating topiary out of many hedges or shrubs that are currently already growing in your yard.

All topiaries consist of several sections called modules. A module is equal to the size of the head of a topiary like the angel, peacock, and duck, and helps keep things proportional. The modules are normally a variation on a common geometric shapes like the ones shown below:

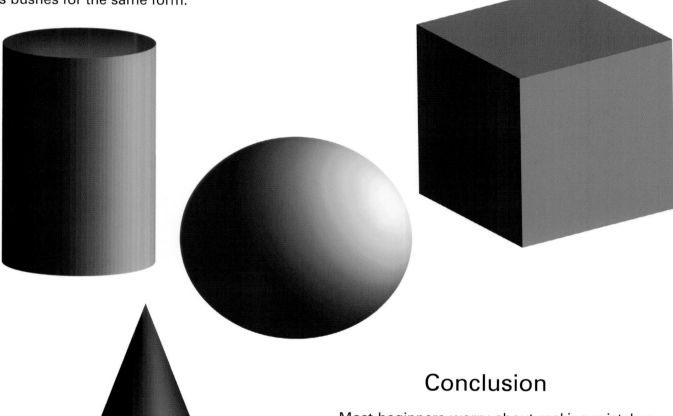

Conclusion

Most beginners worry about making mistakes. They go half way into a project and stop because they get discouraged and give up. Don't let that happen to you. Remind yourself that you are looking at a creation that is incomplete. There is plenty of time to correct any mistakes as you move forward.

This book will give you the foundation on which your topiary will grow. After you construct the basic design you want from your particular bush, you can better develop your design as the bush grows.

I hope this book will be helpful in stirring your imagination and bringing out your creativity. And just think, you can do it for fun or profit!

The Peacock

The plant chosen for the peacock project is an azalea. For demonstration purposes, this is a small plant, but at any size it works well for topiary work. It is a freestanding plant that can be cut fairly rigorously without damaging it. The regrowth will add the fullness and the foliage of the offshoots will fill in the mass. Privet, boxwood, and forsythia also work well.

Assess the value of the plant. If you find any broken pieces, remove them. If you are using an older, larger plant, you will find a lot of dead material in the center. This should be removed before work begins. This old stock will not bend. Wait a month or so for the regrowth to take place before making topiary on these larger bushes.

Rotate the plant to determine the best sides for the peacock topiary. This side is rather sparse at the base…

…which is fine for the back of the figure and the tail feathers.

The opposite side has some lower growth, which is ideal for filling in beneath the head.

Separate the front from the back.

Gather the front section together.

The head and neck are about the top 1/3 of the front. Hold the branches together at that point

Wrap cotton or hemp twine around the base of the head at that point. This will eventually rot away without binding the plant and inhibiting its growth. The green color blends in well.

Pull it tight…

…and tie it off. Leave one end of the twine long.

With the head tied off, the branches are beginning to form the breast of the peacock.

Before proceeding shape the breast a little more, pulling the branches out into a curve…

...and gently sculpting the overall shape.

Add to the long end of the twine.

The long end of the twine is wrapped around the head in a spiral

Continue around several times…

…with the spirals getting closer together as you move toward the top.

Continue all the way to the tip…

…then reverse the spiral and go back down.

When you are about half down to the starting point (the base of the head), push the twine through the branches. This will anchor things for bending later on.

Spiral the twine up again…

Trim off any small frays of twine, leaving the long end intact.

This is a good time to align the head with the breast by giving it a little twist.

…and knot it off about an inch behind the tip.

Put tension on the string to bend the head forward and down, then run the twine through the branches of the neck just below the original wrapping.

...then wrap it around the neck.

Run the long end through the neck again...

Pull it out through the back of the neck through the bundle of branches...

Tie it off, engaging both the wrap and the twine from the head.

...pushing it all the way through.

Trim off any short ends. Again, don't cut the long end of the twine.

Any branches that pop out of the structure...

...can easily be tied to integrate them into the head.

The long end of the twine goes through the "tail" branches.

It should go right though the middle of the back branches, dividing them in half.

If you are working with a container, punch a hole about 2" below the surface.

Pull the twine through the hole.

Pull the twine taut until the head and neck are in their desired position…

…then tie it off.

Cut the excess.

Progress

Tie a new length of twine around the neck and punch a hole in the front of the container, as you did in the back

Move the knot to the back of the neck…

…then run the end of the twine through the body.

Run the twine through the hole, then push the head down to the desired position.

Loop the twine two or three times through the hole and tie it off.

The few loose branches at the bottom can now be tucked back into the body.

Gently insert them into the breast. Because of the structure they will stay there. As the foliage increases, these branches will give mass to the topiary.

Progress.

The piece can be cleaned up at this time, to make it look crisper.

The breast, neck and head are now shaped. As sunlight enters the structure, it will stimulate leaf and branch growth. Let the regrowth fill in the structure before trimming again.

Note: if the plant were larger and in the ground, the twine would be anchored to stakes driven into the soil.

The tail feathers are clustered in an odd number of equally sized groups, at least five or more with larger plants. This gives a center feather and an equal number on each side

Determine the middle group first, locating it right behind the head.

Turn the plant around and make sure you have enough for two or more groups on each side.

You want each feather group to be a little wider in the middle, giving it the shape of a feather.

A few inches from the tip, hold a length of twine in place with your thumb and wrap it around.

Tie it off leaving one long end of twine.

Spiral the long end of twine to the tip…

…then spiral it back a little bit and tie it off.

Spacers are used to shape the tail. They are made of two twigs, taped together in the middle. Their length depends on the particular project. Twigs are used because they camouflage nicely.

Run the spacer through the widest part of the tail feather group from side to side.

The side branches of the tail feather then slip into the gap in the spacer and are held in place.

Tie one end off to secure it, leaving one end of the twine long.

Pull the long end of twine around the back of the tail and loop it around the other end of the spacer.

Bring the twine around the front of the tail...

...and tie it off. The twine will help make the tail flatter.

...then come back a short distance and tie it off.

Divide the branches on one side of the center so they make two feathers. Gather the outermost feather and follow the same steps that you used on the middle feather. Beginning a few inches from the end, wrap it with twine to the end...

Insert the spacer at the widest point of the feather.

Gather the branches into the spacer...

...and tie it off as before.

Because of the wide gap in the base of this feather, a second, small spacer is used to pull the branches together, narrowing the feather base.

...and below. The long twine will be the guy to hold the plant in position.

The outside feather needs to be bent outward, so punch a hole in the container (or drive a stake in the ground) to anchor the twine.

With the spacer in position, use twine to pull the branches together above the spacer...

Insert needle nose pliers through the hole to grab the twine and pull it through.

Tie it off.

This will hold the outside feather in position.

Repeat the same process with the middle feather on this side, tying it...

...and wrapping it spirally to the end.

Again, use a spacer to give it shape.

Tie the middle feather into position. You can use the knot of the previous guy, tying below the knot.

Progress from the back…

…and the front.

Before moving to the other side, tie in some of the straggler branches.

Repeat the process on the other side, starting with the outer feather.

…and continuing with the middle feather.

Align this side with the other so it is symmetrical and tie it in place.

Trim as necessary to make things look neat.

Finished

New growth will occur on the bare wood to fill in the topiary.

A Full-Sized Peacock

In this picture of the peacock, you can see the skeleton of the tail feathers, the body, and the head.

This off season view shows the structure of the head, tail, and breast area. Notice that there is a slight separation between the breast and body. Sometimes topiaries (like this one) require an occasional re-tying or adjusting to pull the sections back together, especially in the spring after new growth. If you are doing topiary as a business, this is where you would make your money.

The leaves on the peacock are re-appearing in early spring.

Full grown peacock.

Peacock to Angel Conversion

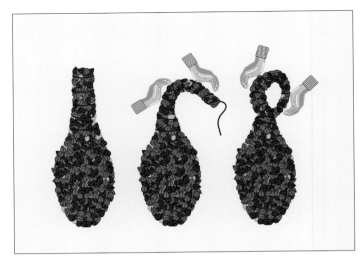

The body and head of the angel is formed in much the same way as the peacock. The difference is that instead of pulling the head forward, it is wrapped in a loop to form a round head. This is shown in this drawing.

A peacock can easily be converted to an angel. Begin by tying a twine to the end of the beak.

Take the twine around the back of the head…

…and pull on the string to turn the head. Hold in place with your forefinger.

Spiral-wrap the head in position…

...and tie in place.

The result. As the new growth fills in, this will become a round angels head.

Turning to the back, cut the ties of the middle feather.

Remove the spacer.

Divide the center feather in half.

Join one half to in innermost feathers on that side, binding the ends…

…and tying off…

...for this result.

Repeat on the other side.

Progress.

Working from the back, and near the bottom, run twine from the back to the front, moving to the right.

Continue through the right wing and bring the twine back to the center and tie. With proper pressure this will bring the wings into position.

Tuck the loose branches into the twine to give it an angel's wing effect.

Progress

When it fills in it should look something like this. As it matures you can add arms with the hands folded in front.

When the foliage grows in, it should look something like this.

The Angel

Notice the structured framework in this photo. Because the leaves are gone for winter, you can see the wings, head, body, and bottom of her dress.

This picture allows you to view the angel from the rear. You can see the wings protrude slightly from behind the head, neck, and upper back of the angel.

This drawing shows how stiff rods worked into the structure help hold the wings in place. The flare of the skirt is made by pulling some branches down from under the wings.

This is a side view of the angel without leaves in the winter.

These pictures show the angel in early spring starting to fill up with new leaves again.

The angel is shown with her new spring growth.

Arms of the angel being trimmed.

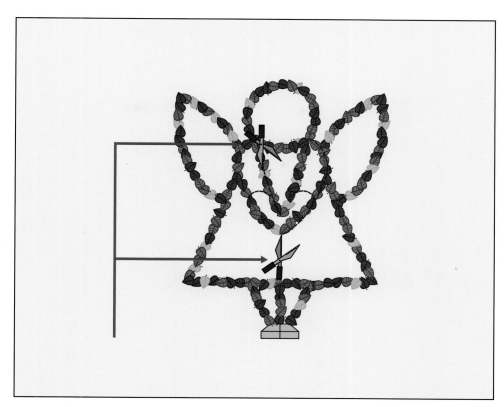

As the foliage comes back, it is possible to sculpt the shapes of the arms and hands using trimmers.

Dress and hemline of the angel being trimmed and defined.

The Gothic Arches

Space the plants evenly apart in the position you like. These are Sky Pencil hollies. Hibiscus or Rose of Sharon make a nice alternative arch that flowers.

Trim the bushes to an equal height.

Tie the twine loosely at the base of the outside plant.

Wrap spirally from the bottom…

…to the top, gathering in as many loose ends of the plant as possible. The end bushes are tight to match the center bushes which will be divided in half before being tied.

At the top, make your spiral tighter, pulling the top to a point.

Divide the second plant in half.

About 6" from the bottom tie the twine around one half.

Again, Make a loose spiral up this half of the plant…

…tightening at the top and tying off

Do the same on the other half, tying near the bottom...

...and making a loose spiral.

Do the same on the next plant.

Continue until you reach the other outside bush, which again is tied with a tighter spiral wrap.

Tie them together at the spot and spiral the twine to the tip.

Join the outside shrub to the nearest half of the next shrub about six inches from the top.

This drawing gives a better look at the joining of the two plants.

Use your body to determine the height of the intersection...

...and carry it to the next shrub connection.

Again tie them at the correct height ...

...and spiral wrap to the tip.

Repeat down the row of plants until you get to the last.

Cut off any twine ends.

The result

A full-size arch in winter

Gothic arches accentuated with spike plants.

An arch in full foliage.

The Duck

The plant is a Rheingold Arborvitae. The more this is in the sun the more the gold color will be enhanced.

Assess the plant. The fullness of this side will do well for the breast and front.

At the other side you need material for the wing and tail.

At the front, pull the plant together to form the neck.

Holding a piece of twine with a finger of one hand…

…wrap it around the neck with the other.

Tie it tightly

After establishing the neck, form the head and beak.

Determine where the head and neck meet…

…and tie it off with moderate tension.

Adjust so the midline of the neck and head are straight and vertical

Make a hole in the container under the neck.

Insert needlenose pliers through the hole.

Pull the twine from the head through the hole with the pliers.

Pull the twine to put tension on the head and bringing it into position.

Tie it off. Wrap the twine around itself at the container to assure a good hold. Then cut off the excess.

Make a loop at the top of the neck where it meets the base of the head. Bring the twine up to the base of the bill and tie. Continue to shape the bill.

Tighten loosely and clip off the excess.

The head was tied loosely so it could be shaped. Hold the twine in place with a finger, then use the handle of the shears or pliers to pull some foliage up to form the top of the head.

Start another piece of twine at the top of the neck under the head.

Gather in some of the loose ends as you wrap it around. Tie it off with moderate tension.

With another piece of twine, pull in the rest of the excess as you wrap around the head. Then tie it off.

Progress.

With the head formed, we can determine how to divide the body for the wings and tail.

Gather the plant at the base of the tail.

Wrap the twine around the tail…

…and tie it off.

With the tail and head roughly formed, the wings are also defined.

Use twine to define and gather together the base of the wing, where it meets the body. Encircle it and tie it off.

Tie it off at the front of the wing with moderate tension. It helps hold the position if you loop the twine a few times before making the knot.

Wrap the long end of the twine around the base of the plant before making the final tie. This will keep pressure on the wing and hold it in the place you desire.

Starting at the base of the wing, make a loose spiral toward its tip.

Work the foliage out to fill in the wing as you go. This will help to hide the twine.

Tie it off at the back of the wing.

Taking the long end of the twine, pull it over the back, pushing the wing in toward the body.

Pull the twine back under the tail…

...and wrap it around the base of the plant.

Come back under the tail and tie it off at the back of the wing, where it started.

Progress. (Above and opposite)

Repeat the process on the other wing. Tie off at the joint of the wing and body with moderate tension.

If your piece of twine runs out, add a second piece. Make it double knot with a lot of tension for long life.

Lightly wrap a spiral around the wing and knot it off at the back.

Pull the wing into the body and loop the twine around the tail and then around the base of the plant. Tie it off.

Tie in the loose breast foliage.

Ready for a final trim (Above and next four photos)

With hedge trimmers clip off the foliage that stands out further than you want. You want to keep as much foliage as possible for fullness.

A duck tail is kind of short and rounded.

When the body is finished, trim and shape the bill.

The finished duck (Above and next three photos)

The same project can be done with barberry and other hedge plants.

When working with barberry it is important to guard against the thorns. Leather gloves are helpful.

Assess the shape of the plant, then use cardboard or wood separate the front from the back.

A bungee cord can be used to temporarily hold the front section. It hooks into the holes at the base of the container.

A knot in the end of the twine is useful when working with a thorned plant.

It enables you to pull the free end of the twine through the loop and avoid tying knots in the thorny foliage.

Pull the front section together and start to wrap it toward the head.

Tie it off at the base of the head. Needlenose pliers will come in handy.

Take the growth available and pull it together to form the head.

Wrap the head in twine. Again, the edge of the shears or another implement can be used to press against the thorny surface.

Pull the head into position, run the twine through a hole in the container, and pull it through.

If you run into hard, old growth, cut it out and wait for the regrowth, which will be much easier to shape.

With these minor adjustments for your comfort, the process is essentially the same.

A Full-size Duck

Pictures of the ducks without the leaves in winter. Seen from the side, back and front, this gives a good idea of the underlying structure. (Above and next page)

A covering of new spring leaves on the ducks will allows an opportunity to better define their shapes.